Provided
by

Measure B

which was approved by
the voters in
November, 1998

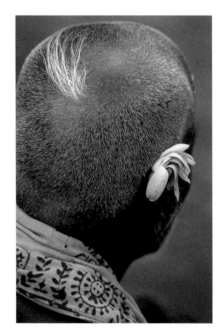

Livingfaith

LIVING FAITH

Windows into the Sacred Life of India

PHOTOGRAPHS DINESH KHANNA

INTRODUCTION PICO IYER

HarperSanFrancisco
A Division of HarperCollinsPublishers

Front cover: Pune, Maharashtra

It is common in India to find everyday objects being worshipped as sacred symbols. Someone from this house, for instance, came upon a stone that suggests the form of Ganesha, the portly god with an elephant's head, and installed it at the entrance.

Back cover: Haridwar, Uttaranchal

Kavadias, devotees of Shiva, are young men from far-flung villages who trek for days to Haridwar to collect water from the holy Ganga river and carry it back home. They walk barefoot both ways.

End papers: Nathdwara, Rajasthan

Sacred symbols of Hinduism painted on a wall

Previous page: Varanasi, Uttar Pradesh

This ancient Peepul tree on Aasi Ghat is visited by hundreds of people every morning and during festivals. The Peepul tree is considered especially sacred in Hinduism. Vishnu, it is believed, sought refuge in a Peepul once when the demons defeated the gods, and Krishna died under one. Some also consider it symbolic of the Trimurti or Trinity: the roots are Brahma, the trunk Vishnu and the leaves Shiva. Buddhists too revere the Peepul as the Bodhi tree because the Buddha attained enlightenment under it.

Facing page: Ayodhya, Uttar Pradesh

Khadauns—simple wooden sandals—are usually worn by sadhus and others who have renounced the world. The Ramayana records that when Lord Rama gave up his claim to the throne of Ayodhya and went into exile, his brother Bharat refused the crown too, and with Rama's *khadauns* on the throne, administered Ayodhya in his name for fourteen years.

Following page: Sonepur, Bihar

Devotees performing a puja that will ensure peace for their ancestors.

For Mahi, Myra, Rachana and Deesh

HarperCollins books may be purchased for educational, business, or sales promotional use. For information please write: Special Markets Department, HarperCollins Publishers, Inc., 10 East 53rd Street, New York, NY 10022.

HarperCollins Web site: http://www.harpercollins.com
HarperCollins®, ®, and HarperSanFrancisco™ are trademarks of HarperCollins Publishers, Inc.

FIRST EDITION

Designed by Bena Sareen

Introduction and all text except for photo captions copyright © Pico Iyer 2004.

Library of Congress Cataloging-in-Publication Data is available upon request.

ISBN 0–06–057823–8

04 05 06 07 08 Tien Wah Pte. Ltd. 10 9 8 7 6 5 4 3 2 1

Colour is what seizes you as soon as you set foot in India, or start paging through the magnificent images collected here: a rich and vital sense of colour, more lavish and more profuse than in any other country that I've visited. The colours grab you as you walk down an Indian street, and speak, it often seems, for a diversity of religions, races and customs more prodigal than in almost any other ostensibly united nation; and they spin you into a kind of aromatic spell in which your senses reel, often, from the intensity of marigolds and saris and decorations on buses, cars and cows. The colours jump off the billboards that line the city streets and then await you as you step into the calm of a village shrine.

Jhalawar, Rajasthan
Worshipping Lord Shiva at the annual festival held on Kartik Purnima, the night of the full moon in the month of Kartik (October/ November), when Shiva killed the demon Tripura.

But colour in India, like everything in India, is not purely an aesthetic thing. It is, like all India's vibrancy, at some level an act of worship, and a proof, for the devout, of the pervading presence of one or many of the country's gods. 'In India art is religion, religion is art,' the great contemporary explorer of belief systems, Huston Smith, said on American television some years ago; which is a way of saying, too, that the ultimate sacred text in India (which is what draws so many visitors from abroad) is nothing but its daily life. The sacred comes to you not only in the churches and temples and shrines that seem to dot every corner of the subcontinent; but through the life that goes on all around them: that figure with palms joined in what an outsider might take to be prayer (offering a namaste to everyone he meets); that woman disappearing into an archway with her daily offering; these men sitting in the local tea-shop debating the purposes and good name of God Himself. Religion is not something tucked away from the world in India, as it often might be in the more secular, recent countries of the West; it suffuses the greetings, the conversations and (notoriously) the animosities of the place.

Dinesh Khanna has travelled around his native land for years now, trying to catch this quality of privacy in India: not just the spectacles and extravagant rites and famous sadhus by which every photographer or tourist who arrives in India is fascinated, but something deeper, and less obvious. India as it goes about its worship alone, largely unseen; India as it exists when there are no cameras around. A place not only of festivals and melas and acts that stretch and challenge the imagination; but a place of regular human beings simply communing with what they believe. The images assembled in this book are caught with a classical eye that can see arrangements and clean lines in even the everyday, and so reproduce the simple elegance of the miniature; but where even the miniature is often consecrated to some public and ceremonial event, the pictures Khanna has collected stir me with their secrecy. He is not saying that faith has been practised or commemorated here, as in the great cathedrals of Europe, around the monuments of Pagan or Borobodur, amidst the temples of Egypt; he is suggesting that it is happening right now, over there, behind that corner, or in the quiet of that room.

Not many years ago, the aforementioned Huston Smith, for me the exemplary religious scholar of our times, published a revised edition of his classic *The World's Religions*, suggesting, with characteristic delicacy, that even though science had arisen in certain places to challenge or refine our sense of the unknowable, it could not push the ineffable out of our lives altogether. Modern Western society, he has said, is the only one that archaeologists have found where a temple is not at the centre of each city (more often, these days, that honour is reserved for a shopping mall, an entertainment complex or a stadium). And progress, as it is narrowly conceived, suggests that the future belongs to the machine, the West, a technology that threatens evermore to cut away the realm of the mysterious.

More recently, Smith, now in his eighties, was moved to bring out a new book called, provocatively (and a little plaintively, perhaps) *Why Religion Matters*. His assumption now was that our belief in gods, our respect for worship, even our faith that there is some providence that shapes our days and confers on them a kind of order have all come under particular and new assault because of all the crimes that have been committed of late in the name of religion. This is nothing new in human history, of course (history could even be defined as the story of all the injustices and atrocities performed in the name of gods, or a better world), but it has taken on a new urgency at a time when a few radical Muslims have attacked the very centre of 21st-century society, the World Trade Towers in New York, and America has retaliated with talk of a crusade. In Kashmir, in Sri Lanka, in the Middle East and northern Ireland, as much as in the days we comfortably call 'barbaric', people are still slaughtering one another daily on the basis of religious divisions and using the name of peace-loving teachers to brand everyone else an 'infidel'. Much of the world believes that God is dead; much of the rest of it holds, worse, that He is a murderer, for sanctioning a humanity that, in ostensible pursuit of the good, violates every commandment in its holy books.

It's no surprise, perhaps, that if we are looking for an image of the all-seeing and the all-knowing nowadays, something that stands beyond our understanding and seems

Palitana, Gujarat
A *sadhvi* (nun) meditates outside a Jain temple. Jain sadhus and *sadhvis* have no home; but for the four months of the rainy season, they must always be on the move, always on foot. The *sadhvis*, like the sadhus, wear white and are bald: since shaving is forbidden, each hair is plucked out meticulously.

as close to infallible as we can imagine, we more likely turn to our Power Books (the scientist Stephen Wolfram has recently published a magnum opus, *A New Kind of Science*, in which, inverting Einstein, he argues that the entire universe is a kind of computer, and to that extent something infinitely knowable). While religion offers no solutions, blinking machines, very often these days, seem to have all the answers.

In India, though, this elimination of the sacred has not yet been completed. India teems with the software engineers who have made many of our computer breakthroughs possible, it bubbles over with financiers who are far from allergic to the profit motive, and it is for many people the epicentre of religious intolerance: fifty years after the horrors of Partition, Muslims and Hindus are still killing one another on its streets and trains while every season brings some new religious war, in Amritsar, in Gandhi's own state of Gujarat, in the heart of Mumbai. Some people might understandably wish that religion were not such a living force in India. And yet on a private level, individually, something else is taking place. Indeed, private acts of worship and devotion may be, more and more, how people try to cope with the larger forces unleashed by people taking the name of

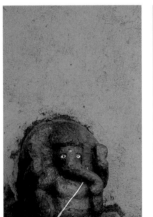

No corner or niche is too small for the gods: shrines built into walls in *Haridwar (Uttaranchal)*, *Pune (Maharashtra)* and *Nathdwara (Rajasthan)*.

religion in vain (after the attack on New York there was a sudden rush in America for books of consolation and every religious figure moved in to the breach as doctors might after an accident). Private faith is how we try to make peace with or take shelter from all the terrors involved in collective religious practice, with its divisive sense of 'us' against 'them'. One of the things that moves me in Khanna's pictures is that they concentrate relatively little on grand events of mass worship; at almost every point he seems to pick out the individual, going his own way, with his own concerns, trying, in the turmoil all around, to separate himself from the mob and claim a small moment of peace and petition. (Clearing a quiet space amidst the bombardment of India is not the least of the achievements of this photographer's sensitive eye.)

In that sense, India becomes a model for tolerance of a kind. It is, after all, home to many of the world's great monotheisms, cradle of its most visible polytheism, the place where the founder of its great non-theism (if that's what you wish to call

Nathdwara, Rajasthan
'Shubh Labh', which translates as 'auspicious profit', is traditionally painted at the entrance of shops and offices along with a representation of Lakshmi, the goddess of wealth, or Ganesha, the remover of obstacles.
Kolkata, West Bengal
Chillies and lime are hung at the doors of homes, shops and offices to ward off evil.

Buddhism) was born. Jains and Jews and Sikhs and Syrian Christians all have found a home there. The most famous living Buddhist practitioner—the Dalai Lama—has lived for most of his life as a guest in India, and India has now become the centre of Tibetan Buddhism worldwide. The world's most admired Catholic, Mother Teresa, did her work here, continuing a tradition that has left many Indians (to the surprise of foreigners) with the names of John and Thomas. India is the home of the Many, but many of them are in constant communion with the One. When you look at Khanna's pictures—and this is often true for a foreigner walking through India's streets—what strikes you is not the difference between all these creeds, but some deeper kinship: in all of them an individual retreats from the world, if only for a moment, to talk to whatever he or she considers Absolute. It may have a name different from that of her neighbour's divinity, but it doesn't need to have a name at all. The terms she happens to give it are the least important thing about the object of her prayer. I sometimes think of Mumbai, for example, the hometown of both my parents (one from Tamil Nadu, one from Gujarat), and the place where many of my relatives, regardless of their religion and background, live even today. For many of us Mumbai is a counter-Varanasi of a kind, Mammon's largest stronghold on the subcontinent, the focus of India's love of cash, its fascination with the new and the Western, its criminal populations and black markets, its prostitutes and even Bollywood that has mixed together devotion and lasciviousness to create a kind of raucous secular religion. Mumbai seems to stand for the opposite of whatever values—of clarity, of stillness and of fellow feeling—religion might seem to offer us; it is the clamour of the bazaar mixed with the commotion of a big city where five million people live on the streets, spiced with the most gaudy of our consumerist or criminal aspirations.

And yet, for all its recent Fundamentalist outbursts, Mumbai still sits in the world's imagination as a model of collective tolerance of a sort, where more religions have lived more harmoniously together than almost anywhere; in some respects, London and New York take their cues from Mumbai. Salman Rushdie, no friend of religion (and one of the most conspicuous individual victims of it, when the Ayatollah Khomeini placed a death sentence on him for his fiction), constantly returns to his hometown, Mumbai, in his writings, to find images of pluralism and forbearance to take back to his new homes, in Britain and the U.S.. Rohinton Mistry, sitting in Toronto for thirty years, goes back to a single small area in Mumbai to find images of humanity and real compassion. In his most recent novel, *Family Matters*, one of Mistry's characters even suggests that Mumbai's trains could serve as a beacon for the world: every time one pulls out of Churchgate Station, leaving a few latecomers running after it, those on the train will reach down to try to pull the

Jaipur, Rajasthan
Women string marigold and rose garlands to sell to devotees outside a temple.

stragglers up, regardless of whether they are Hindu or Muslim or Jew. Such distinctions don't matter when a human is simply reaching out to another human with an extended hand.

Mistry is far too great a realist (and he knows India far too well) to let that hope go unchallenged. The action of his novel in fact shows how quixotic that hope often may be—the idealist who formulates the image

Nizamuddin, Delhi
Sufism in India has many similarities with the Bhakti movement of Hinduism that flourished in medieval times. The emphasis in both is on devotion: the devotee follows the path of surrender to his god, who is seen as the divine lover or 'husband', to whom ecstatic love lyrics are sung. This similarity, coupled with the humanism and compassion of Sufi saints, has also made Sufism popular among Hindus. At Sufi shrines like the *dargah* (tomb) of the thirteenth-century saint Hazrat Nizamuddin Auliya in Delhi, many Hindus come seeking fulfilment of their deepest desires.

gets killed by the forces of intolerance, and Fate is always about to deal one of the Parsee characters another hardship. Nothing is ever quite so easy as our better selves would wish. And yet the point nonetheless remains: if too much idealism is fatal, so, too, is too little. However rarely people—or religions—live up to our best notions of them, they never conform wholly to our worst expectations, either. And living in the single most multicultural city in the world, Toronto—in a country universally respected for its peace and tolerance—Mistry nevertheless returns to Mumbai for (in all senses) inspiration.

When I go back to India, even now, I always make a trip to Dharamshala (and have done so since 1974). Partly, of course, because one of the world's great religious presences and spokesmen for tolerance and ecumenicism, the Dalai Lama, is living there, meeting with Jews, speaking on the Gospels, sharing ideas with hardened atheists and agnostics. But even more because Dharamshala is as strong an image of living faith and quenchless devotion as I have seen. The few thousand Tibetans who live on McLeod Ganj, a small ridge above the main town of Dharamshala, are nearly all refugees, from a culture that has seen all but thirteen of its 6,254 monasteries destroyed, more than a million of its people killed and its monks and nuns imprisoned, forced to copulate in the streets and made, at gunpoint, to eat or destroy sacred texts. If there is any place where religion has been assaulted almost to the point of destruction, by pragmatism and godless modernity, it is Tibet. And yet here in India the Tibetans pray more devoutly than any people I know. They come to the Namgyal Temple at dawn—many of them barely able to walk— and turn its great prayer-wheels. They put a light to the long rows of candles that stand in front of the snowcaps in the distance—and, as the day goes on, watch young monks practise classic dialectics as if they were in one of the great monasteries of Lhasa. Every day new refugees arrive, having made a treacherous trip over the Himalayas, for many weeks, just to set eyes on the man they regard as the embodiment of their living faith, and to come into contact again with the source of their inspiration. A small Tibetan settlement in what used to be a British hill station, filled more and more with the young people of Japan, Israel, America and Europe, is not what most of us think of when we think of religious practice in India; and yet it is one of the latest, 21st-century incarnations of a spirit that seems changeless in the subcontinent, which somehow contines to be fertile ground for whatever affims the old, the unseen and the deep (in Tibet itself, of course, many of the monks you see today are spies or informers, and the ones who chant sutras in the street are generally asking for handouts). The Tibetans in recent years are finding what the Zoroastrians found when they fled Iran hundreds of years ago, and what Jews have found, and the Catholic sisters of Mother Teresa: that amidst all the divisions broadcast in the headlines, private worship (and acts of kindness and devotion) remain as potent in India as anywhere on earth.

The first time I looked at the images collected here, I was struck, as many viewers might be, by their sense of design combined with their feeling for everyday humanity; by their ability, in a way (and India's ability), to find a moment of worship and devotion at a crowded street stall, or leaning up against an old car. Yet the more I looked at them, the more something else began to happen to me, something deeper. I felt I could hear the shuffle of feet along the corridor where that old woman is sitting in prayer. I could smell the quiet of that morning where two figures are walking along a country road. I could hear the gong that was being sounded where that boy was whirling himself into an ecstasy, and could feel the silence around that man as he stepped down the steps of Varanasi to a ghat. Something mysterious happens as you lose yourself in these images, and it is a something that has a lot to do with India, but a lot to do, too, with a photographer who has steeped himself so deeply in its murmured prayers and chants that it is as if he has disappeared inside the people he portrays, and now can give us their hearts from the inside out. His, too, is a living faith, you realize, of patience and attention and surrender, which allows him to get into the scenes he finds and then have them speak back to us.

The meaning of 'religion', it's always important to remember, is 're-binding'; at its heart it is a force that brings us together into something greater than ourselves (it is only a human distortion of religion that makes it divisive). That is close to one meaning, too, of course, of yoga, the Indian discipline that is so popular now in America and Australia and Japan. What Dinesh Khanna has done in these pictures is, I think, something of what India does, at its best: namely, to take individual moments of worship, private acts of devotion—the soul in solitary colloquy with its God—and somehow bind them into the larger fabric of society and life. It is something that is easy not to see when you are wandering around India's event-filled, swarming streets, and it is something that few foreign photographers would be able to penetrate deep enough to register (you have to live with these moments for a long time, I suspect, to be able to bring them back to us, as delicate as a soapbubble carried across a river). Yet if you listen closely enough to them, you can hear, I think, the voice that speaks, mumbling through prayers, when no one else is around. And at a few moments, you can even hear the voice that replies.

PICO IYER
Nara, Japan

The Silent Moment

One person alone in a crowd, lost to the world and given up to some world far beyond herself. Silent in the middle of the clamour, not even recognizable to herself any more, or her friends and family; taken out, for a moment, from whatever lies in the moment and brought into close contact with whatever stands beyond it.

There is water everywhere in these pictures of quiet ceremony, and there are the ageless props of flower and fire and fruit; more deeply, there is a sense that, in prayer, the smallest things—a hat, a coconut, a single thread—become transfigured and take on more meaning than they would ever have otherwise, as a candle does. The act of worship consecrates everything it touches, so that even a simple bowl becomes a receptacle of something deep.

In Agra, only two weeks ago, I found myself outside a mosque where vendors were thronging around tourists, boys were chattering furiously and every step I took was attended by unwanted companions ('No, sir, please, sir, I am not salesman. Student only!'). Then I stepped into the shrine of a Sufi saint, and everything was still. Just a man murmuring a brief chant, another, hands extended, eyes closed, in silent prayer, some women scattering petals across a cloth. Prayer, the act of worship, takes a passing moment, something small, and makes it last forever.

Previous page: Lucknow, Uttar Pradesh
Lighting incense at the Karbala, a Shia shrine.

Facing page: Sonepur, Bihar
A woman on her way to the Ganga to make offerings to Surya
(the sun-god) on the morning of Chhatth, Bihar's biggest festival.

This page: Omkareshwar, Madhya Pradesh
A woman on the banks of the Narmada river with a *lota* full of consecrated water.

Kolkata, West Bengal
A worshipper says her prayers to the departing Goddess at the end of
the annual Durga Puja festival. The nine-day festival concludes with
the immersion of Goddess Durga's idols in a river or lake.

Varanasi, Uttar Pradesh
Yoga and prayers on the ghats of the river Ganga.

Palitana, Gujarat

Pilgrims at one of the 1,008 Jain temples in Palitana. Before entering a temple for worship, Jain devotees usually change into red and yellow unstitched clothes.

Patna, Bihar
Anointing symbolic representations
of local deities.

Amritsar, Punjab

A Sewadar (a devotee who does voluntary service) at the Golden Temple, the holiest shrine of the Sikhs. Also known as Harmandir Sahib, it was built during the time of the fifth Sikh Guru, Arjan Dev. The Guru invited a Muslim Sufi saint to lay the foundation stone, for Sikhism was initially a synthesis of the Hindu and Muslim faiths. The Golden Temple has doors on all four sides. Guru Arjan Dev is believed to have said: 'My faith is for people of all castes and all creeds, from whichever direction they come and to whichever direction they bow.'

Amritsar, Punjab
A woman praying at the entrance
to the Golden Temple.

Junagadh, Gujarat
Unusually for a mosque, this one
has exuberantly colourful interiors.

Lamayuru, Ladakh
An old Lama at the Lamayuru Gompa
(monastery).

Lamayuru, Ladakh
Watching the Lamas dance at the Lamayuru
Gompa festival. The hat and prayer beads are
an essential part of the traditional attire of
Ladakhi Buddhists.

Kurukshetra, Haryana
A pilgrim meditates at the *mela* (religious fair) held in
Kurukshetra during a solar eclipse. Ancient texts describe
Kurukshetra as a town situated on the central line of the
universe, and bathing in its sacred tanks during an eclipse,
when the sun, the earth and the moon are also in a straight
line, is thought to ensure moksha or salvation.

Haridwar, Uttaranchal
A sanyasin, prayer beads in hand, waits
for her train at the railway station.

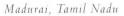

Madurai, Tamil Nadu
Several shrines around the country have a tradition of childless couples
making offerings to the presiding deity or saint in the hope that their wish
for a child will be fulfilled. At this temple devotees tie miniature cradles to
the tree in the courtyard, with an idol of the infant Krishna in them.

Kanchipuram, Tamil Nadu
A stylized representation of Ganesha.

Facing page: Sonepur, Bihar
Making offerings to Lord Hanuman, the
monkey-god.

Palitana, Gujarat
Pilgrims among the 1,008 Jain temples on the sacred
hill in Palitana, one of the holiest places for Jains.

Velanganni, Tamil Nadu
People tie threads and locks for wish fulfilment,
a practice more common in Hindu and Sufi
shrines, outside a church.

McLeod Ganj (Dharamshala), Himachal Pradesh
A Tibetan woman prays at the wish-fulfilling
Kalpataru tree. The message on the tree is
about the disappearance of the Dalai
Lama's successor in China.

Velanganni, Tamil Nadu
Devotees at the Basilica of Our Lady
of Health. It is a tradition here to offer
a candle in the shape of the ailment the
devotee suffers from—a red heart-shaped
one for cardiac complications, yellow
candles shaped as lungs in the case of
tuberculosis, and so on. If the devotee is
cured, the Virgin Mary and the church are
thanked by offering a silver replica of the
part of the body that was diseased.

McLeod Ganj (Dharamshala), Himachal Pradesh
This small hill town in northern India has been
home to the Dalai Lama and the headquarters of
the Tibetan Government-in-exile since 1959.
The present generation of Tibetans, many of
whom were born here, may have adopted
contemporary dress and ways but their faith
in Tibetan Buddhism is alive and strong.

· 53 ·

Nizamuddin, Delhi
Copies of the Quran and other sacred texts of Islam are kept for
the benefit of worshippers in mosques and Sufi shrines.

Thanjavur, Tamil Nadu
Lamps and fire are
central to every Hindu
ritual of worship.

Thanjavur, Tamil Nadu
Praying at the
Brihadishwara Temple
dedicated to Shiva.
The sculpture at the far
right depicts Shiva as
Nataraja, dancing the
Tandava (the cosmic
dance of dissolution
and regeneration).

Udipi, Karnataka
A priest offering consecrated water
to a devotee as prasad.

Lucknow, Uttar Pradesh
The main prayer area at the Karbala, an important
place of worship for Shia Muslims.

Spituk, Ladakh
The austere life of the
Lamas is mirrored in
the stark architecture
of this monastery built
atop a hill outside Leh
in the eleventh century.

McLeod Ganj (Dharamshala), Himachal Pradesh
A Tibetan Buddhist monk with his prayer wheel and beads.

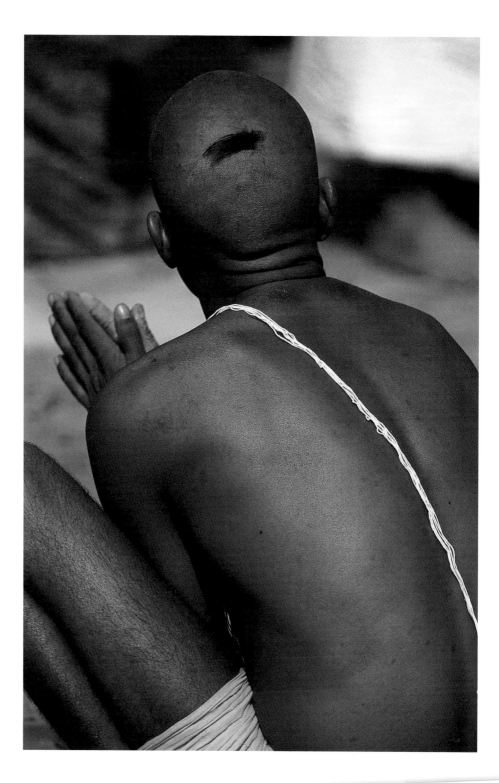

Allahabad, Uttar Pradesh
A Brahmin at the Kumbh Mela. The head has been shaved
and the hair offered for the well-being of his ancestors.
A tuft of hair, known as a *bodi* or *shikha*, is retained, a
common practice among devout Hindus, especially
Brahmins. Many upper-caste male Hindus also
wear the *janeu*, a sacred white cotton thread
that signifies their caste status.

Young pilgrims having their morning glass of milk outside the Sri Meenakshi Temple, *Madurai, Tamil Nadu* (opposite page); a pilgrim, carrying a blue plastic idol of the Virgin Mary with the Infant Jesus, in the compound of the Basilica of Our Lady of Health in *Velanganni, Tamil Nadu* (this page). Shaving of the head and offering the hair to the deity is a common practice among Hindus in Tamil Nadu and Andhra Pradesh that has been adopted by many Christians as well.

Pune, Maharashtra
People too busy to queue up for a glimpse of the deity in
the temple make their offerings to this image outside.

Nashik, Maharashtra
Worshipping Hanuman, armed with his mace,
depicted vanquishing a demon.

Shinganpur, Maharashtra
Praying to Nandi, the gentle bull. Nandi is Shiva's *vahana* or vehicle and also his
insignia. An image of a seated Nandi is usually found in front of a Shiva linga
(the phallic representation of Shiva) and devotees often touch its loins and flanks,
seeking both its strength and restraint.

Varanasi, Uttar Pradesh

Varanasi or Banaras, Lord Shiva's city, is the most ancient living city in the world. Dying or being cremated here is supposed to guarantee moksha—liberation from the cycle of birth and rebirth. The cremation is handled by an outcaste called Dom, while the officiating priest, a Brahmin pandit, stands apart.

Chidambaram, Tamil Nadu
Early-morning puja at the tenth-century Nataraja Temple
dedicated to Shiva in his Ananda Tandava pose (the Cosmic
Dance of Bliss). Brahmin priests perform the elaborate
puja dressed in traditional white dhotis.

Puri, Orissa
A devotee offers his prayers in the midst of
jostling crowds at the Jagannath Rath Yatra.

The Sacred Space

Living faith in India takes place in living colour; you can attach almost any adjective you like to the subcontinent, but the one word you are seldom apt to use is 'dead'. Everything is moving, pressing together, drifting off again, and yet at some level nothing is ever changing—the way a colour reflects the sun in all its passing movements, becomes different every moment of the day, and yet tomorrow, at dawn, is shown to be very much what it was at dawn this morning.

It's easy to feel, on first encountering India, that there are so many sacred spaces that they swallow up everything, make every space sanctified in a way. The crowded shops, the garlands hanging from the mirror of an auto-rickshaw, the stone Ganesha by the street, the Virgin peering out from a sea-going vessel: every square inch, it can sometimes seem, is given over to some object of veneration, even if it is no more exalted than a Hollywood goddess.

A part of India's magic, I think, is that it draws together so many cultures and centuries: you will find the high blue heavens of Tibet, the madonnas of Europe, the designs of the Arab world and even the shrines of cyberspace wherever you turn in India. Jains, Jews, Syrian Christians, all are practising their forms of worship, with the result, sometimes, that India seems to teem with gods. And yet, most happily and importantly, they are always in the very midst of mortals.

Previous page: Mangalore, Karnataka.
Mango leaves at the entrance, to ward off
evil, welcoming words on the door and the
auspicious Tulsi plant in the courtyard are
found in most traditional Hindu homes
around the country.

Nizamuddin, Delhi
Tabizes for sale outside Hazrat
Nizamuddin Auliya's *dargah* (tomb).
A *tabiz* is an amulet containing a sacred
charm that is to be tied around the
neck or the arm.

Varanasi, Uttar Pradesh
A symbolic image of Hanuman
carved into a wall.

Jaipur, Rajasthan
While the world hurtles on, there is always time
and space for the sacred, as for this devotee at a
shrine by the side of a busy road in Jaipur.

Varanasi, Uttar Pradesh

Facing page: Varanasi, Uttar Pradesh
A Peepul tree, which has grown roots
right through the wall, becomes a
small temple.

Thanjavur, Tamil Nadu
The entrance to the Brihadishwara Temple to Shiva,
one of the World Heritage sites in India.

Velanganni, Tamil Nadu
The Roman Catholic
Basilica of Our Lady of
Health is an all-white
neo-gothic structure.
People of all faiths visit
the church during the
annual nine-day festival
that celebrates the birth
of Mother Mary.

Udipi, Karnataka
Most older Hindu temples have a sacred tank
where devotees bathe, especially on festival days.

Jodhpur, Rajasthan
The blue wash on this temple is typical
of most buildings in Jodhpur.

Udaipur, Rajasthan
A small shrine under a
Peepul tree by Lake Pichola.

Chhatarpur, Delhi
Visitors to the Chhatarpur Temple make a
wish and tie handkerchiefs and *chunnis* to
this tree in the compound.

Nashik, Maharashtra
A temple on the banks of the river Godavari, also known as
Dakshin Ganga, the Ganga of the South. Several temples
along the river attract pilgrims throughout the year.

Goa
Small Hindu and Christian shrines
and Crosses dot the landscape of Goa.

Mount Abu, Rajasthan
The Guru Shikhar temple, on the highest peak of the Aravali range,
dedicated to Dattatreya, an incarnation of Lord Vishnu.

Tikse Gompa, Ladakh
Spartan single-room quarters of the Lamas, where they lead
a secluded monastic life. Gompa, which is what a Buddhist
monastery is called, translates as 'solitary place'.

McLeod Ganj (Dharamshala), Himachal Pradesh
The Dip Tse-chok Ling Gompa with its yellow roof
gleaming through the wood cover.

Benaulim, Goa

Calangute, Goa
A statue of Madonna outside a church.
Goa, ruled by the Portuguese for over
450 years till 1962, has the
largest population of Roman
Catholics in India.

Haridwar, Uttaranchal
Built by traders from Bengal, this temple also serves
as an ashram where sadhus and pilgrims can stay.
The architecture is typical of the havelis of wealthy
merchants in Bengal made during the early 20th
century. The unabashed use of the colour red,
considered auspicious in Hinduism, makes this
one of the most distinctive buildings in Haridwar.

Haridwar, Uttaranchal
A man meditates in the compound of the Bengali Ashram.

Details from temples in *Ayodhya* and *Varanasi, Uttar Pradesh*

Madurai, Tamil Nadu
Part of the Thousand-pillared Hall in the Sri Meenakshi Temple
dedicated to Meenakshi, an incarnation of Shiva's consort, Parvati.
The accurate number of the carved pillars in this hall or *mandapam*
is 985. Just outside the hall are the famous 'musical pillars', each
of which, when struck, produces a different musical note.

Varanasi, Uttar Pradesh
A spot for worship at the base
of a gigantic Peepul tree.

Nagapattinam, Tamil Nadu
Snakes, especially cobras, along with cows, are
considered the most sacred animals in India.
They are worshipped for fertility and the welfare
of the family. Snake worship was probably an
ancient animistic ritual that was later absorbed
into the mainstream Hindu faith.

McLeod Ganj (Dharamshala), Himachal Pradesh
An aged devotee spins the giant prayer wheel
at the Namgyal Temple. The prayer wheel
contains scrolls with Bodhisattva (Enlightened
Being) Avalokiteshwara's mantra 'Om Mani
Padme Hum' repeated several times. Tibetan
Buddhists believe they earn special merit by
spinning the prayer wheel. Each clockwise
revolution is equivalent to chanting all the
mantras contained in the scrolls once, and
earning an equal number of blessings.
The same principle applies to the small
handheld prayer wheel.

Hemis Gompa, Ladakh
A young monk in the kitchen of the monastery.

Kolkata, West Bengal
Most commercial vehicles like taxis, trucks and buses have small shrines in them to the gods the driver believes in. A puja, complete with incense sticks and flowers, is performed before the first journey of the day.

Kanchipuram, Tamil Nadu
Holy markings on a truck tyre made by the driver, perhaps to ensure safe passage on India's treacherous highways.

Goa

Most boats in Goa have images of gods, goddesses, prophets and saints painted on them. These could be Christian or Hindu. The two communities in Goa share many similarities in the details of their rituals, iconography and music, which are largely inspired by ancient folk traditions.

Previous page: Ganga Sagar, West Bengal
Images of the presiding deity of Ganga Sagar up for sale along with
posters of rock and film stars and female WWF wrestlers.

Madurai, Tamil Nadu
God is omnipresent. Nowhere is this more true than in India. Street
corners, traffic intersections, the trunk of an old Peepul tree can all
accommodate a small shrine.

Facing page: Kolkata, West Bengal
No Hindu ritual of worship or an auspicious occasion like a
marriage is complete without flowers and garlands.

Brindavan, Uttar Pradesh
A miniature shrine, complete with
little doors that are shut when
it is time for the deity to rest.

Brindavan, Uttar Pradesh
Houses down a lane in Brindavan, Lord Krishna's hometown.

Into the world

Religion bursts into the streets again, in India as everywhere, in great festivals and celebrations and acts of strength. Men flagellate themselves along the roads, gods float in the waters, the faithful show off their guns and devotion. In some ways India represents not just the practise of religions, but the consequences, sometimes the horrors, of clashing faiths and rites; one group asserts itself at the expense of others, and the moment of silent communion turns into a show of mass force.

It is not possible, of course, to contemplate the power of religion without taking in the shadow side of that strength, and seeing that the worship of gods remains, alas, a human, all too human thing. The nature of humanity is to fail to live up to the possibility it is always celebrating.

Yet India instructs us constantly in the joy and colour and vibrancy of reminding ourselves of our faiths, and of affirming whatever lies beyond us (or, some would say, inside us). The dance along the beach, near otherwise highly irreligious Mumbai; the sudden appearance of a groom, transforming the streets around him with his act of ceremony: is it any wonder that the Kumbh Mela and a hundred other festivals in India remind us that faith is a chant, a surge and a throng? The living, the dead, the gods and humble mortals, all swirl together around us in the practise of a faith until you laugh and you shout and you look a little closer—and you notice, at the corner of one eye, a tear.

Previous page: Ajmer, Rajasthan

The *dargah* or tomb of the twelfth-century Sufi saint Khwaja Moinuddin Chishti, also known as Khwaja Gharib Nawaz (The Benefactor of the Poor), is one of the most revered shrines in the Indian subcontinent. During the annual Urs, which commemorates the death anniversary of the saint, millions of people of all faiths from India and Pakistan come here to pray and offer *chaddars* or sheets.

Anandpur Sahib, Punjab

Nihang Sikhs in Anandpur, the site of an enormous fair during Hola Mohalla. The festival was started in the early eighteenth century by the tenth Sikh guru, Gobind Singh, as a gathering for military exercises and mock battles. The Nihangs were originally warriors whose duty was to defend the Sikh faith from the armies of the Mughal empire. To this day a Nihang is easily recognized by his traditional blue or yellow dress, his martial demeanour and the arms he always carries on him—swords, spears, shotguns and even pistols.

Omkareshwar, Madhya Pradesh
Triangular saffron or red flags are often seen atop
Hindu temples and around other religious sites.

Omkareshwar, Madhya Pradesh
Of the five elements, fire is integral to almost all
Hindu rituals, whether during daily prayers at
home or community worship at a temple, as in
this one on the banks of the river Narmada.
Omkareshwar is one of the twelve Jyotirlingas
in India, sites where Shiva is believed to
have manifested himself.

Nizamuddin, Delhi
The qawwali, a beautiful legacy of the Sufi faith in India, is a musical
offering to God. The lyrics are always in praise of Allah and express
the poet's and singer's desire to merge with the Almighty. In Delhi,
there is no better place than the mausoleum of the Sufi saint
Nizamuddin Auliya to experience the magic of the qawwali.

Varanasi, Uttar Pradesh
There are certain times of the year that are considered most
auspicious for weddings. This leads to situations like this one,
where more than one marriage party—*barat*—may be passing
through a narrow lane at the same time.

Puri, Orissa
A dancer at the beginning of the Jagannath Rath Yatra. In the
background is the main chariot with the image of Lord Jagannath
that will be pulled through the streets by thousands of devotees.

Juhu Beach, Mumbai, Maharashtra
Ganesh Chaturthi, dedicated to the elephant-headed god Ganesha,
the remover of obstacles in every enterprise, is the biggest festival
in parts of western and southern India. Idols of Ganesha are
displayed in homes, offices and in public spaces for a week, and
on the seventh day they are taken to be immersed in the sea or a
nearby river. In Mumbai, especially, traffic comes to a standstill.

Kolkata, West Bengal
Durga Puja, the nine-day festival celebrating the slaying of the demon Mahishasura by Durga, the mother goddess, is the highlight of the year in Bengal. Large clay-and-straw statues of Durga are set up in every neighbourhood and business comes to a complete halt in the entire state for these nine days. The climax of the festival is the immersion of the statues in the Hooghly river.

Previous page: Velanganni, Tamil Nadu
A *mithai* (sweets) shop does brisk business outside
the Basilica of Our Lady of Health.

Bidar, Karnataka
Offerings for the deity at a shop outside a temple. Austerity is
rare in places of community worship in India.

Facing page: Patna, Bihar
A typical early-morning scene on the banks of the river Ganga
in Bihar. Everything happens together: the washing of clothes
and bathing of buffaloes continue even as people perform
their prayers and take a dip in the holy river.

Pushkar, Rajasthan
Pushkar has the only temple in the world dedicated to Lord Brahma, the
Creator. During the Pushkar Mela, which is held on the full moon of
October/November, hundreds of thousands come to take a dip in the
Pushkar Lake and trade in camels and horses.

Chidambaram, Tamil Nadu
Brahmins performing their ritual prayers and bath at
the tank of the ancient Shiva temple in Chidambaram,
the City of the Cosmic Dancer (Shiva).

The Living Encounter

In China, in Japan (where I live), in many of the Eastern cultures that I know, you seldom see signs of worship in the street; rites are for the temple (or the home) and the thoroughfare is for the things of the world. In the West, too, religion is generally practised, when it is practised at all, in the spaces set aside for it. India does not believe in such false distinctions, however: a sadhu is sitting outside a mandir in Karnataka and a pilgrim is having lunch over there. Jain nuns are walking along a road, passed and swerved around by racing bikes, and a swami is presiding over a pavement fish stall. The shaven head and the holy book are everywhere.

That sense of ubiquity—of life within every nook and detail—is one of India's great lessons to the world, I think; religion is not confined to the temple or shrine here, but is taking place on that coughing bus, or along that sidewalk where people are living and, too often, dying. Religion is, in fact, only as potent as its place in the human drama. The priests of India often take us aback by not being as pristine and otherworldly as we would wish them to be; the people of India often take us aback by seeming as pious or philosophical as priests. The pilgrim teaches us, in effect, that every step is a step towards a holy place, and the roadside wise man teaches us that every moment is, if seen right, a holy moment. The Ganges shows us that living faith in India continues into and through even death.

Previous page: Tirupati, Andhra Pradesh
The traditional, and most important, offering at the Tirupati temple is a person's
hair. Both men and women have their heads tonsured here. Tonnes of human hair
are collected every week and sold to manufacturers of wigs in India and abroad.

Chidambaram, Tamil Nadu
Collecting flowers for the morning prayers from a Laburnum tree.

Jhalawar, Rajasthan
Pilgrims at the fair held on Kartik Purnima, the day of the full
moon in the auspicious month of Kartik (October/November).

Spituk, Ladakh
It is a tradition among the Buddhists in Ladakh
to send one child of the family, usually a son,
to a monastery to become a monk. So one
normally sees a large number of young boys
living the austere and disciplined life of a
Lama in Ladakhi monasteries.

Kanchipuram, Tamil Nadu
A novice priest in the temple city of Kanchipuram,
one of the seven most sacred cities of Hinduism.

Omkareshwar, Madhya Pradesh
Pilgrims cook their meal on the ghats of the Narmada river.
The Narmada, according to legend, was created by Shiva from a
drop of his sweat to deliver the earth from a terrible drought.
There are numerous pilgrimage spots by the banks of the
Narmada. Some determined pilgrims undertake the arduous
Narmada Parikrama, a circular pilgrimage on foot along
the entire course of the river that lasts over three years.

Velanganni, Tamil Nadu
It is a tradition among Hindus, especially in Andhra Pradesh
and Tamil Nadu, to get their heads shaved while on a
pilgrimage. Here, interestingly, Christian pilgrims do the
same at the Basilica of Our Lady of Health.

Mathura, Uttar Pradesh
A devotee in Lord Krishna's
birthplace.

Madurai, Tamil Nadu
One of the entrances of the Sri
Meenakshi Temple.

Kolkata, West Bengal
A single red chilli at a fish-seller's stall to
ward off the 'evil eye'.

Kolkata, West Bengal
A marigold flower on the weighing scales: a
vegetable-seller's offering to the instrument
of his trade.

Kolkata, West Bengal
Gods watch over a pavement fish shop.

Varanasi, Uttar Pradesh
Whole families sometimes come on a
pilgrimage to Varanasi. Many live on the
ghats, where they set up makeshift kitchens.

Varanasi, Uttar Pradesh
A flower bazaar near a temple.

Mumbai, Maharashtra
The Mount Mary Church in Bandra has an annual
festival during which people offer wax models of things
that they want God to grant them—from
computers to houses, and guitars to aircraft.

Velanganni, Tamil Nadu
An important feature of the annual festival at the
Velanganni Church is the bazaar where images of Christ
and the Virgin Mary are sold along with watches,
sunglasses, saris and much more.

Puri, Orissa
Pilgrims take a meal break during Lord Jagannath's
Rath Yatra, a rare private moment while the
journey of the deity's chariot continues
outside in the crowded streets.

Varanasi, Uttar Pradesh
Early morning on the ghats.

Maheshwar, Madhya Pradesh

A priest dresses up Lord Hanuman's statue after its daily morning bath. Hanuman, the monkey-god, son of the wind-god, is a celibate with enormous physical strength and is especially revered by wrestlers. Unlike other male gods of the Hindu pantheon, he is rarely depicted dressed in a dhoti. He wears a loincloth, the preferred garment of wrestlers. It is believed that he was born with this loincloth (*kaupina*), which is a symbol of his chastity.

Kolkata, West Bengal
Men brush their teeth with Neem twigs alongside the Devi
statues they sell by the banks of the Hooghly river.

Kumbh Mela, Allahabad, Uttar Pradesh
A sadhu catches up with worldly matters. The Kumbh Mela attracts millions of
pilgrims and tourists from India and abroad; it is as if a whole new city comes up
by the banks of the Ganga where different eras seem to co-exist: naked sadhus
from the Himalayas with almost no contact with modern civilization walk
among technocrats from the great metropolises of the world.

Haridwar, Uttaranchal
A sadhu who lives under a Peepul tree by the banks of the river Ganga. A bag, with all his worldly possessions, including a *chillum* to smoke *ganja* or hashish (a common practice among sadhus), hangs from his *trishul* or trident.

Kurukshetra, Haryana
A Shaivite priest, his forehead adorned with the sacred mark of the *trishul* (trident), the weapon of Lord Shiva.

Agra, Uttar Pradesh
A woman in a trance-like state at the *dargah* (tomb) of a Sufi saint near the Taj Mahal. In numerous small shrines of different faiths all over India, people believed to be possessed by spirits are brought by their families to be cured, and sometimes to be abandoned.

Varanasi, Uttar Pradesh
Dharamshalas in temple towns offer very basic
but cheap accommodation for pilgrims.

Ganja, or hashish, is closely associated with
Lord Shiva, the supreme ascetic, and it is
common practice for sadhus to smoke it.

Puri, Orissa

The giant wheels of the *rath* or chariot of Lord Jagannath
(literally, Lord of the Universe) at the temple in Puri. During the
annual Rath Yatra festival, the enormous chariots of Lord
Jagannath, Balabhadra and Subhadra are taken out in a procession
and hundreds of thousands of devotees throng the streets to pull
the chariots along, for it is believed that this will earn them
moksha, liberation from the cycle of birth, death and rebirth.
The English word 'juggernaut' derives from this festival.

Varanasi, Uttar Pradesh
An old man returns home from the river with a *lota* full of *Ganga jal* (holy
water from the Ganga) after performing *Surya namaskar* (ritual prayers to
the sun) on the ghats. *Ganga jal* is used in all purification rituals. Some
Hindus, like this man, use it to purify their homes every morning.

Patan, Gujarat
Jain *sadhvis* (nuns) walk barefoot from one holy place
to the other, virtually on an eternal pilgrimage. There
is great emphasis on non-violence in Jainism, which is one of the
reasons why the monks and nuns never use footwear: they are less
likely to hurt a living creature like an ant when walking barefoot.

Varanasi, Uttar Pradesh
A woman and child
sleep on the terrace of
their home surrounded
by temple spires.

In India, a country with over a billion people, it is common to see crowds and congregations, especially in places of worship or during festivals and religious fairs. And there is often a temptation to treat people as an amorphous mass, or worse still, a mob. But crowds are made up of individuals, each with her own beliefs, each in direct communion with her Maker, even when surrounded by thousands of others.

It is this private faith that I have come to value most of all and hope to celebrate through the images in this book, especially at a time when, increasingly, the more visible face of religion is prejudice and intolerance.

—*Dinesh Khanna*